making christmas happen

Daily reflections to help you keep the sparkle in all the preparations

kevin mayhew

First published in 2006 by

KEVIN MAYHEW LTD
Buxhall, Stowmarket, Suffolk, IP14 3BW
E-mail: info@kevinmayhew.com
www.kevinmayhew.com

© 2006 Susan Sayers

The right of Susan Sayers to be identified as the author of this work has been asserted by her in accordance with the Copyright, Designs and Patents Act 1988.

All rights reserved. No part of this publication may be reproduced, stored in a retrieval system, or transmitted, in any form or by any means, electronic, mechanical, photocopying, recording or otherwise, without the prior written permission of the publisher.

Where stated, scripture quotations are from the Holy Bible, New International Version, copyright © 1973, 1978, 1984 by International Bible Society. Used by permission of Hodder & Stoughton, a member of the Hodder Headline Group. Otherwise, quotations are paraphrased by the author.

9 8 7 6 5 4 3 2 1 0

ISBN 1 84417 669 X
Catalogue No. 1500936

Cover design by Sara-Jane Came
Edited and typeset by Katherine Laidler

Printed and bound in Great Britain

CONTENTS

INTRODUCTION

Who tends to organise the cards, gifts and decorations in your household? Who does most of the shopping and prepares the Christmas meal? And all those millions of other jobs that have to be done if Christmas is going to happen?

Are you involved, by any chance?

This book is specially written for the busy people who spend their weeks before Christmas doing a wonderful job of preparation. Exhausting sometimes, yes, but well worth it when you see the faces on Christmas Day.

Making Christmas Happen gives you a short, daily reflection to help you keep the sparkle in all the hard work, and hold on to the real wonder of Christmas.

It follows the jobs you will be doing anyway, like sending the cards, buying and wrapping the gifts, putting up the decorations, going to the carol services, and preparing for the Christmas meal.

So it shouldn't feel like yet another job to fit in, but more like a glass of wine and a mince pie to keep you going along the way. Hopefully you'll arrive at Christmas Day feeling a little more refreshed by your Advent than usual, and able to enjoy the festivities with extra sparkle.

Use it on your own or with a group, as there's plenty to set you thinking and encourage you through Advent.

SUSAN SAYERS

WEEK 1

CARDS AND GIFTS

DAY 1

Keeping in touch and losing touch

I wonder who you have added to your Christmas list this year? And who have you decided or, sadly, have had to cross off? That list represents something of our current circle of family and friends and so could be a kind of prayer list throughout the year.

For some of those on it we hardly need the list, because we know them so well and are in regular contact, so there's no way we would forget them or accidentally forget to give them a card or present. You may well be one of those people on someone else's list, and have the good sense of belonging and being often in their thoughts. Be thankful in your prayers for this close circle of family and friends. It's all too easy to take for granted those around us, and yet if you just imagine for a moment how barren and lonely life would be without them, the thankfulness will come pouring into you freshly again. Paul starts his letter to the Christians in Philippi like this: 'I thank my God every time I remember you' (Philippians 1:3, NIV).

Do we let our family and friends know how thankful we are for them? Perhaps we assume they know, but actually it does feel really uplifting and reassuring to be told at regular intervals. When we spend a lot of time with our loved ones we can easily get out of the habit of giving them our full eye-to-eye attention without any other agenda than enjoying and delighting in them. Somehow all the rushing and stress of life crowds out one of the most precious gifts we have for this journey between birth and death: the companionship of loved ones. That's a God-given blessing which we all too often treat so casually and carelessly.

How about voicing some of that thankfulness more often? Sending the Christmas cards and choosing and wrapping presents is at least one time in the year you can put your love in writing.

As you prepare the Christmas cards and gifts this year, how about also making a point of looking sometimes into the eyes of those you love, with love and thankfulness and pride in your heart for them? Don't worry if they don't seem to notice at first – we often don't notice what we aren't expecting to see. But relationships need maintenance just like anything else, and if we slip out of this 'taking for granted' mode, we'll find it starts having a wonderfully restoring and positive effect. We will find ourselves appreciating our loved ones more and better able to cope with all the ordinary scratchy times which there are always bound to be.

Pray for your loved ones as you write the messages in their cards or the round-robin Christmas letter. Pull back the spending budget so that choosing the gifts is not filled with anxiety but becomes a pleasure again. Think about the words you put on the labels, so that the words become part of the gift.

God looks at us with eyes of love and we are always close to his heart. God notices all the little hurts and slights we have to put up with and all the happy contented times we enjoy. God knows about our funny ways and our irritating habits and the reasons we behave the way we do. But none of that makes God love us less because, along with every other human person, we're in that close 'family and friends' circle as far as God is concerned, and God loves us with tender affection.

Spend a moment of quiet in God's company and you'll start picking up on those intimate and affirming encounters when God whispers his love into our hearts. Start noticing all the gifts and cards God sends us to express his love in the world around us as well – sunsets and raindrops, bare branches against a clear sky, the colours and shapes of flowers and fruit and vegetables in the shops, warmth when we get indoors out of the cold wind. All things bright and beautiful! They are God's way of whispering, 'I love you'. We can enjoy those messages of God's love and we'll find our relationship with God deepening just by accepting his gifts and living more thankfully.

We probably all have people on our Christmas list whom we've almost lost touch with completely. As we all move on or move away, it's impossible to keep up with everyone, and although we have fond memories of times we've spent together, there simply aren't enough hours in the week to meet regularly any more. But that once-a-year contact through the Christmas card is very important. It affirms the good friendship we value, and holds the door open so that we know we'll be able to get in touch again and pick up the strands easily and comfortably.

Sometimes our relationship with God can get to the occasional card or visit stage. God stays there on our list perhaps for years without very much contact on our part, and because of God's courteous nature he will never gatecrash where he isn't invited. That picture by Holman Hunt of Jesus as the Light of the World, standing outside and knocking on the door of our heart, has truth in it.

Of course, the perception that cultivating a friendship with God is a time-consuming extra, which we can't fit in to our important schedule, is a false perception that leads us into a spiral of stress. By neglecting the one thing that truly gives us peace and satisfaction, we wear ourselves out by more and more time-filling and worry. Jesus advises differently. 'Seek first the kingdom of heaven,' he says, 'and then all the rest will be added to you as well.'

So rather than us not having the time for keeping in touch with God, the truth is that we'll only have time for everything else if we *do* keep in touch with God! God will then gradually realign our priorities, heal us of the need to prove ourselves acceptable or valid or lovable, and free us up to live with lighter hearts. It makes you wonder why we all take so long to realise what is such a happier way of living. But there you are – we're human and find it hard to trust very good news.

I can remember a time in my life when I buried my cross and Bible deep in the recesses of a junk cupboard but something stopped me from actually throwing them out. I suppose that was like having God there on my Christmas list but making a deliberate point of not getting round to sending the card. And I remember searching through that cupboard years later to find the Bible and cross and bring them out. It felt a significant moment in my faith journey.

If this is for you a time of renewing your acquaintance with God, well, you've chosen such a beautiful season to do it! As we get ready for Christmas with all our preparations, you can now put God at the centre of your list of loved ones and perhaps write God the first Christmas card, thanking him in your prayers for all your blessings, and expressing to him that, yes, you love him and are much looking forward to getting to know him better. And you'll find God's love starts washing through every other card you send and present you give, so that your whole circle of family and friends has extra sparkle.

DAY 2

Expectations and disappointments

The temperature of expectations shoots up at this time of year. Its fire is stoked by all the advertising designed to persuade us that we need particular products urgently and nothing else will do. Collectively we play the Christmas game, working up to an ideal of Christmas which bears very little resemblance to the actual possibility. You see the anxious desperation in people's eyes and jaw lines as they pound the high street, searching. It's hard to avoid being caught up in the pre-Christmas frenzy of expectation, but there are ways to protect ourselves from this and start enjoying the preparation time again.

This Advent let's stand back from all that a moment and catch our breath and regain our balance. And let's start with ourselves and our own expectations. What is it you are hoping to get for Christmas this year? Now don't start laundering your first thought about that in case it isn't holy enough for an Advent book! God can only work with us to the extent that we are honest, and so there's not much point in pretence where God is concerned. There's nothing wrong in being who you are, because that's the person God already knows and loves.

What you are secretly hoping for is probably directly linked with your nearest and dearest and how you would like to be treated by them. There may be a sense that all the responsibility for Christmas being 'successful' always falls on you, and you are a bit apprehensive about that and wish there was more shared labour. There may be the flash of a dream you have almost given up on and have become skilled at shutting away because it never gets fulfilled. Perhaps there is a special something you are hoping will be picked up and acted on, but experience has taught you to avoid expecting anything in order to avoid the subsequent disappointment.

If any of this touches a nerve with you, bring it to God right now and let it sit there unwrapped in front of you both. Recognise where it's coming from and what it looks like, and commend it to God. Give God permission to deal with it in the very beautiful way that only God can, and then wrap it up carefully and put it away again.

Several things might happen as a result of this. One is that God knows our deepest 'wants' in the sense of our needs, and responds to those rather than our greeds. For us it isn't always easy to work out which is which, but now God will be working on that discernment for you.

You may find that those genuine wants will be provided for, though possibly not at all in the way you had expected. You may find that something you had thought was a greed, so that you were ashamed of naming it, was actually a want which God is able to heal and provide for, now that you have acknowledged and voiced it. Often in the gospels we find Jesus asking people to voice their need as part of their healing. ('What is it you want me to do for you?' 'Lord, I want to see.' Mark 10:51)

Or you may find that God starts healing your perceptions, so that priorities subtly change and thankfulness cleans away the crusty residues of resentment which you've been living with for a long time. Whatever it is, relax about it now in the knowledge that God's will happens and you can leave it up to him.

Then there is the 'hardening of the oughteries' which can seriously damage our joy. If we become too specific in our view of what ought to happen, and how things ought to be done, we are setting up the disappointment ready to collapse on us and reinforce a kind of chronic discontent. So what can we do about that?

Perhaps we need to learn from water the art of flowing and taking on the shape of the place it finds itself in. The character of water is not threatened by this ability to be flexible, and we too don't need to worry that we are under threat by other people's ideas being as valid as ours, and their way of doing things different from the way we have thought of. Diversity is a Godly characteristic, as we can see clearly from the diversity of God's creation, and if God enjoys all the richness of variety, then so can we, without wanting to impose our particular methods on to everyone else. So try giving the 'oughts' a Christmas off this year.

As you plan who is going to be at whose home this year and negotiate the treacherous path of everybody's expectations, pray for God's grace to do that negotiating in a Godly way. As families grow and extend, the expectations will need to change shape – other people are brought into the picture and families have to learn to take turns in the 'who goes where' game. Most of the disappointment comes from a lack of communication, so keep talking and check that everyone involved is up to date with the latest plan, so that you avoid the hurt and upset of 'well, nobody told *me*'. And if that happens accidentally, put it right sooner rather than later.

If other people's expectations of you are unrealistic, talk about it and make it clear what you can and can't give and do, rather than killing yourself or bankrupting yourself to meet impossible expectations. Some disappointment is all a healthy part of life's pattern and if something is difficult to say now, it's not going to get any less difficult if you leave it.

When the religious leaders had false expectations about what the Messiah would be like, Jesus refused to align himself with those misguided ideas. He was scrupulous about letting people know the truth, even though he knew it would challenge and disappoint them. What was needed was not a changed Messiah but healed expectations.

So let God heal your expectations, both in the little things and in the big stuff about life and faith. Ultimately, we need to put our trust in the One who will never let us down, who knows our needs, not just now but also for the future, and is interested in our eternal good because he loves us (Psalm 146). 'Seek first the kingdom of God and his righteousness, and all the rest will be added to you' (Matthew 6:33).

DAY 3

Wanting to please

Part of loving is wanting to please. It is because we are fond of someone that we want the best for them and love to put a smile on their face. We enjoy doing or giving something that makes them see we have thought carefully about them and got in touch with their needs. As we plan the cards and presents for particular loved ones, we imagine them enjoying whatever we are planning, with their lives made a bit easier or their day brightened by our gift. Giving is beautiful, and whenever we give out of love like this we are actually behaving 'in the image and likeness of God' (Genesis 1:27).

With such a lot of giving out of love at this time of year, there is a real possibility of our jaded human relationships taking on a communal sparkle, and often that is exactly what people notice about the Christmas season. We call it the Christmas spirit and it can melt congealed hearts, cut through impossible deadlocks and be a tender place of healing. It happened famously between the trenches in the First World War, and happens in less public ways in communities wherever people get inspired by the joy of giving and pleasing another.

Catch yourself giving out of love and wanting to please. Notice it, enjoy it happening, and thank God that you are created with this Godly hallmark of generous, thoughtful giving. Not only are you behaving like God when you do it, but you are also giving God a present. You see, there is nothing God enjoys more than watching his children behaving at their most beautifully human, so God delights in you as you delight in pleasing another.

John wrote about this in one of his letters to the early Christians: 'No one has ever seen God; but if we love one another, God lives in us and his love is made complete in us . . . Whoever lives in love lives in God and God in him' (1 John 4:12, 16, NIV).

Of course, God's nature is also to please out of love. Jesus obviously enjoyed the beauty of the wild flowers, the grandeur of mountains, the refreshment and cleansing of water, the power and gentleness of wind and waves, the warmth of friendship and shared food, the light and darkness, colours and sounds. As followers of Jesus, we are glad to be materialistic – in the sense that the created world is good and a gift to be treasured and enjoyed. Even when life is very painful for us, God will often show us something beautiful to lift our spirits and give us hope.

How lovely that we can return the compliment and support one another in the same way. Choosing a card to please someone is quite a little thing really, but it can lift someone's spirits and make them happy. Is there anyone not on your Christmas card list at the moment who perhaps doesn't have family and would find a card from you a real blessing? Or is there anyone for whom a short visit, or help with writing or posting their cards, or an hour of baby-sitting, might be an answer to prayer?

Being part of the body of Christ is about being family in a new way which goes beyond the natural family boundaries. Your brothers and sisters stretch around the world and God's hope for us is that we will love one another as family.

Consider gifts which will bless in a wider way than simply pleasing the person you are giving to. There are quite a few catalogues around now enabling you to give gifts which provide fresh water or goats or tools. Look at fairly traded options as well, so that indirectly you are pleasing and blessing whole communities. There are also possibilities for wrapping up a shoebox full of gifts for a child or a whole family in another area of the world and bringing a smile to their lives. All the age groups can join in the fun of this kind of giving, and it is such a good training in unselfishness to choose gifts to give rather than get. Even very young children can learn through this the joy of giving without expectation of receiving in return, so that the 'wanting to please' is the priority.

And as you get to the stage of posting your cards and wrapping your gifts, pray for each person. Think of wrapping up a token of your love and thankfulness for them, and pray that as they open the parcel or envelope they will be opening up a message of your love together with the love of God.

Let all your Christmas 'wanting to please' speak into your heart about wanting to please God in the way you live all the year round. What are the kinds of gifts from you to God which would put a smile on God's face, do you think? Take a moment to reflect on that. I wonder what it is that you are already doing or saying or thinking in your day-to-day living which makes God happy?

Perhaps you can see how doing some of the same things but in a slightly different way would be like adding that extra sparkle to your giving to God. Like keeping your giving more secret perhaps, so that only God knows the sacrifice involved. Or doing things more thankfully without grumbling. Or saying less and listening more during phone conversations. Or remembering to thank God when you are delighting in the gifts of God's world. Or being less critical of others who lack your stamina or enthusiasm.

I suppose it all comes down to spending quality time in God's company, because then we're far more likely to pick up on what makes God happy, and we'll also be available to hear when he plants good ideas in our hearts and asks us to give them to someone else with his love.

DAY 4

Giving and receiving

'Freely you have received, freely give.' (Matthew 10:8, NIV)

Yesterday I was really low on fuel and realised I had stupidly left my wallet behind, so there I was with no money to buy petrol to get home! A kind friend lent me a ten pound note and I carefully filled up to £9.99, wary of risking going over and not being able to pay. As I handed over my ten pounds and was given my penny change, I was very conscious of my giving being possible only because of my receiving.

Of course, the truth is that everything we have is like that ten pounds, and the kind friend who gives us the means to give to others is God – which makes us happy and humbled both at once. It amazes me, God's kindness and generous love. It amazes me whenever God has clearly noted my need and responds through someone else or a remembered word of Jesus, or a series of coincidences, or fresh resources of patience and perseverance.

God gives to us on a daily basis – in fact, on a moment-by-moment basis. All the intricate fine-tuning of the universe and all that makes life possible is gift. It is an extraordinary gift that you and I share the privilege of a span of consciousness between birth and death which we know as 'life'. That gift enables us to bless others through our living, with the resources available to us combined with the exercise of our wills to choose well and our hearts to love with mercy.

And in the transaction a mysterious transforming takes place. Our thankful receiving of the gift effectively unwraps it to reveal its shining qualities. This is no ordinary living, but life in full abundance, lit up and shining with the light of God. As the hymn has it, 'The love of Jesus, what it is, none but his loved ones know.'

The gift is activated by the receiving, so that the receiving becomes the gift.

Then, when we give generously out of that abundance, the transforming carries on, spreading out in all directions and bringing hope and healing to the people we meet and talk to, and into the situations we pray for, so that the world is blessed and the gift becomes the receiving.

How good are you at receiving gifts? It's quite a skill and some of us find it difficult to be at the receiving end. We feel much more comfortable doing the giving. This may be to do with a learned guilt about enjoying receiving, because of the 'more blessed to give than to receive' quote, so perhaps it's worth saying that Jesus didn't mean receiving was therefore wrong and something to refuse at all costs. After all, he asked for a drink at the well, he asked for the disciples to support him in prayer, and he was looked after on his travels by that group of women named in Luke's gospel.

As we've seen, sometimes the best gift you can give to someone is receiving happily from them. That allows someone else the joy of giving, and it trains you in humility, because when you receive from someone else you put down your power over them and are willingly placing yourself in a position of openness and vulnerability. And if we don't get into the habit of happily receiving from other people without protesting, we shall find it hard to receive from our heavenly Father without protesting, trying to pay for the gift in some way. We can become driven people if this condition is chronic, and we need God's medicine.

What God prescribes for the condition is very simple and very difficult! Do you remember how angry Naaman was when he was instructed to wash seven times in the river Jordan? He found it all very insulting to his high position and refused until his friends pointed out that it was worth giving it a try. And when he humbled himself – by following those simple instructions and swallowing his pride and high-handedness – his skin disease was completely healed.

So I would encourage you to put in some practice with the joyful humility of receiving. And don't you dare try to pay for the gift in any way. Naaman did that too. If you do, you will be effectively taking away the gift you have just given by receiving. Do you know, that urge to rush in and pay back is a sure sign that you can't bear to be indebted to anyone. You can't stand grace. In which case, there's another area of healing identified. Don't worry, God can do that healing and he understands why you need it. Just hand it over and thank God that he has suddenly shown it up to you. As I write I too am praying for your healing.

How good are you at giving? Do you sometimes shrink from giving in case it gives messages of commitment which worry you, or in case you don't get it right, or in case you might unintentionally be unfair to someone? Or do you feel inside that the other person won't really be wanting a gift from someone like you? It takes quite a lot of self-confidence to give, and if we know our own self-esteem is not strong, present-giving at Christmas can be quite a stressful activity.

Be encouraged by the way Jesus does his giving at the feeding of the five thousand. What was available seemed pathetic, but to Jesus it was plenty and some left over. So much blessing for so many, from one young person's offering! Join forces with Jesus and think of yourself giving out of God's resources as well as your own. You are in the role of the disciples who trotted about between the groups on the grass distributing the gifts of fish and bread as Jesus continued to bless God and break the bread and fish. The pressure is off, and you are free to enjoy the actual giving as God's messenger.

And as you enjoy the giving, seeing the people benefiting from God's gifts, so God will be healing you and building you up in confidence through his love for you. That's another gift!

DAY 5

Counting the cost

Christmas is a costly business, isn't it? It's a big spend time for us, and retailers and credit card companies bank on our willingness to pay out more than is sensible. Along with the spending comes the financial debt monster which threatens to knock us off balance and stop our sleep. And what on earth has all that got to do with a baby laid in a feeding trough because there was no room at the inn?

You may well be in the middle of all that spending at the moment, anxious about making ends meet and yet wanting to give generously and provide your family and friends with the things they really hope to get. When are we going to come to our senses and take back control of this outsized spending which does nothing to enhance the celebration of Christmas but rather has the adverse effect of making people dread it and long for it all to be over?

Why not make this the year when you do something about it? Instead of running after the balls all over the court, take control of the game and start calling the shots yourself. You can do this as an individual, as a family, or even as a church community, deciding to celebrate Christmas in style, but in a style that frees people from the financial headaches.

There are various ways of doing this. You can agree in your circle of family and friends on a really low ceiling amount for presents, for instance. Make it clear that the presents are little tokens of love and thankfulness, so in a way the 'what' is not so important. And they can still come beautifully wrapped and with special messages on the labels. The bonus of this is that there is suddenly a wider choice of gifts available, and the buying or making of the presents becomes altogether more fun. Somehow the 'tokens of love' approach allows us to focus more clearly on why we are buying gifts for one another anyway.

Another way of addressing the problem is for everyone to draw a name out of the hat and just buy one present. Or pool the money for a charity gift and join the children in preparing some simple homemade presents. Church communities will sometimes have one huge card that everyone writes their messages on, together with a collection box so that money can be given to charity. Or there may be a display area for everyone to give one card to the whole church, rather than all the individual ones.

It's harder, of course, to make these changes when there are children and young people in the full force of spending expectations and at risk of being laughed at or despised for belonging to a family which is 'different'. It helps if a group of families or a whole church community takes a stand together, perhaps in partnership with a charity such as Christian Aid, so that the 'less is beautiful' encourages everyone involved. There is a real gift in this for many households who loathe the debt but can't see how to avoid it and stay acceptable.

Whether or not you change Christmas giving dramatically, do review your finances and budget properly so that you are not letting the pressure to spend get in the way of the real Christmas focus. To simplify doesn't mean that you will be shutting Christmas out. It will actually enable you to celebrate more.

All this is a real challenge to us about what Christmas is for. Much of the hype is reclaiming the Pagan festival of Yule, with its celebration of the days beginning to get longer again after the solstice on 21 December and the prayers for a full and fertile growing season ahead. It was this light in the darkness and hope for new growth and lengthening days which the Christian Church decided to use for celebrating the birth of Jesus, the Light of the World.

So now, what are you, as a Christian, wanting to celebrate? Rather than buying in totally to the Yuletide festival under the Christmas heading, perhaps we need to use our money to reflect what we are really celebrating. And that will have more of a noticeable effect on our finances than anything else.

Think in terms of love coming as a person: of God laying aside his majesty and humbly choosing to share our human nature in all its ordinariness. Think of Mary giving birth after days on the road and away from her home. Think of the news being told to the shepherds – social outcasts because of the nature of their job, dealing with blood and birth and death, and unable to keep religious festivals properly. Think of wealthy wise ones opting out of their comfort zones and kneeling in the dust to offer their mysterious gifts as signs and sacrifice. Think of Joseph taking on the responsibility of protecting this baby and his mother in dangerous times.

And if any of that jars with any of the items on your Christmas list, consider crossing them out and thinking again about the best and most authentic way to celebrate Christmas. Then lay your wallet, your credit card and cheque book down in front of the crib and offer your spending power back to God.

DAY 6

The greatest gift of all

This week we have been accompanying our preparing of cards and presents with some reflections. Today is a little different. I wonder if we could spend this time looking at the greeting and the gift which God was preparing for us at the first Christmas and is preparing for the end of all time, at what we sometimes call 'the second coming'.

Think yourself back to the moment before creation. The Bible describes a sense of chaos and lack of form or order rather than a blank nothingness (Genesis 1:1). Like a huge pent-up energy of possibilities without any shape or purpose. But God is already there. What kind of universe will he choose to create?

Suppose the birth of Jesus speaks a prophecy back into this moment and forward to the end of all things? Suppose the Christmas event starts right here, at the birth of creation? If it does, we might expect there to be in the kind of creation God chose such things as an extraordinary humility and laying aside of power and majesty, a central and absolute commitment to love as the meaning, and a voluntary vulnerability.

And do we find those qualities in the created universe we know as home? Yes, I think we do.

One of the deepest cries of human hearts is an agonised wrenching 'Why?' as each generation witnesses pain and suffering and struggles to match that with a God of love. It makes no sense and looks like a cruel joke, or proof that God is a sham.

Unless . . .

Unless we look at creation in the way we look at the manger. Could it be that God chooses a manger kind of vulnerability in the whole fabric of the created order, a manger kind of commitment to love, whatever the cost and danger, and a manger kind of humility?

If so, we might expect a universe where God in humility allows the very creation to become instrumental in how the universe develops, with an acceptance that this will not be following a rigid programme but be surprising and varied and creative, with possibilities, failures and successes, and redeeming and transforming all built in. What a shocking humility to lay aside control voluntarily like this, laying down instead only the kind of laws we choose to call physics and chemistry. But also what a beautiful, courteous and honouring humility, leaving us and all the created order with privilege and responsibility, and a dynamic authority under God.

We might also expect a universe where the commitment to love is total, whatever the cost. And since love requires that we choose freely, there is a dangerously heavy cost, since we must also be free to choose not to love. We are all acutely aware of that cost. We experience it ourselves and inflict it on others. Both directly through our own wrong choices and indirectly through our refusal to speak out against wrongs which need righting, we add to the cost. But we also know that God is right to have built in that freedom because it means we can pour out our love to one another and to God, so that we are able to experience all the joy and abundant life that God has in mind for us.

And we might expect a universe where God considers it more important to share vulnerability alongside the unfolding creation and his people than to return the creation to chaos by constantly interrupting the laws of gravity or the cooling crust of a planet.

Both through the creation and through the manger, God's gift is to be there right with us in the pain, suffering and danger, as well as all the joy.

So as we also prepare ourselves for the folding up of the earth and the heavens as we know them, and an accomplishment of all that has ever been planned in the heart of God, perhaps the hallmarks of that final day will be nothing other than the beauty of humility, vulnerability and love, which brings total healing of all hurt and pain, an enabling of all that is good and true, and a profound recognition from the whole of creation that Love empowers, redeems, transforms and has the ultimate victory.

So the gift that God is preparing for us is also the gift he has already given us, both in Jesus at Bethlehem and also in our very nature as members of the created order. It is a gift reflected in those gifts of the wise men: gold, frankincense and myrrh.

Gold is formed through the creative pain of the planet's cooling, so it speaks to us of the way suffering, conflict and destruction can become places where something of lasting beauty and purity is forged. Frankincense gives off its fragrance as it is burnt, and so speaks to us of self-giving humility, that willingness to relinquish our selves in order to serve. And myrrh puts us in touch with the painful and yet liberating truth of our mortality – our vulnerability and the fragile nature of this planet and our universe.

DAY 7

Something to think, something to pray and something to do

Something to think . . .

Why am I sending these cards and buying these presents?

Something to pray . . .

Here I offer you, Lord Jesus,
all my preparations for Christmas.
Teach me more about giving
and more about receiving.
Realign my priorities
in tune with your will,
and enable me to see more clearly
how best to celebrate your coming
as our Lord and Saviour.
Amen.

Something to do . . .

1 Make your cards and presents preparation into opportunities for prayer, giving thanks for your loved ones, and asking God's blessing on their lives.

2 Plan to make this Christmas reflect your real celebration, rather than allowing yourself to get drawn into the irrelevant expenses and expectations.

3 Set aside moments to wonder at the beauty and humility of the greatest gift of all.

WEEK 2

DECKING THE HALLS

DAY 1

Clearing the clutter

I'm not exactly fanatical about clearing clutter. It amazes me how after clearing those papers and bits and pieces once, you turn your back for a moment and there it all is again – clutter sidling into your life uninvited and making itself comfortably at home.

But one of the times I make a point of a good clear-away is this time of year, before the Christmas decorations go up. If I'm honest, I think I probably panic that if the decorations and cards are put on top of the clutter, I might really lose the plot! And anyway, there's something about clearing out before Christmas which feels like a useful form of preparation at many levels.

What do you think of as clutter? Is it a bit like weeds – simply wild flowers in a place you don't want them? Is it your in-tray which happens to be shaped like a living room? Is it everybody else's stuff trespassing on your patch? Is it hard copy of an over-full life? Is it a recycling sack without a sack, which you can't bring yourself to throw out? Is it time you don't have, waiting to be available? Is it a monster to keep out or a pet to relax with?

Whether you are a 'comfortable with clutter' person, a 'maddened by clutter' person or a 'clutter – what's that?' person, let's look at some pre-Christmas de-cluttering in a spiritual sense.

Spiritual clutter accumulates in our soul and from time to time we need to look at what's there and get rid of anything we would be better without. A bit like hitting delete on all that junk mail. We also need to install some kind of anti-virus programme to block unhealthy clutter from clogging up our spiritual life.

What might spiritual clutter look like, and how do we recognise something as clutter?

In the parable of the sower (Luke 8) Jesus describes some of the seed of the word of God falling among thorns. This, said Jesus, 'stands for those who hear, but as they go on their way they are choked by life's worries, riches and pleasures, and they do not mature.'

In our culture life's riches and pleasures are certainly not seen as thorns. Rather the opposite – having plenty of money is good, highly commendable, and something to encourage. And as for pleasure, no one questions that – all we have to do is check that the quality and quantity of our pleasure is properly monitored and in line with health and safety regulations. Instead of it being clutter, we are supposed to clear away anything which prevents us from making lots of money and having top-quality pleasure. Even life's worries are regarded as part of the package, with the pleasure and money offsetting the inevitable stresses. Life's worries, riches and pleasures are not perceived as thorns but more as seeds.

St Francis was brought up in quite a wealthy home and took riches, worries and pleasures for granted until he came to view them as clutter. At which point he couldn't wait to get rid of them and embrace 'Lady Poverty'. He could see that sometimes what the world commends clutters us up and prevents our spiritual growth. He also saw that it is the possessive way we think that is the problem, rather than any particular item or dream.

Anything that gets in the way of you having a deeper experience of God is probably clutter. That means that ordinary, commendable things or ideas may turn out to be clutter if you have grown a bit possessive about them. It may be that you need to clear not the actual things but your possessive or defensive attitude to them.

One way of checking your junk is to think through the way you spend your time and money in a typical week. Do it in the light of what Jesus said about those thorns of worries, riches and pleasures. How much time is your mind on those issues? How much is your spending geared to addressing them?

Instead of buying into the story we get fed through advertising and the media, buy into the quiet whisper of Jesus speaking about different priorities altogether. And if your attitude or lifestyle jars with what you are hearing, you are faced with some choices to make.

Either carry on as you are, with your spiritual growth getting stunted and the likelihood that you won't mature spiritually, or swap the worldly values for Godly ones and look forward to a spiritual growth spurt. You might expect the choice to be easy but I don't think it is. Those attitudes have deep roots and we like what we have grown accustomed to. The choice is bound to involve some kind of sacrifice and none of us likes giving up what we find enjoyable, comforting or supportive.

What I have found, though, is that if we ask God for the strength and courage to do something like this, it doesn't come *until* we make that decision bravely on our own. It's like the way people keep putting off having children until they can afford it – that day will never come, however rich they get. What really happens is that when they badly want to have the children, their perception of what financial position is necessary changes.

Look at the advantages of freeing yourself from those thorns and clutter. Don't worry about them, don't run after them, Jesus says, because they aren't the necessary, lasting things that will give you peace of mind and real joy. Instead, Jesus suggests we change our priorities and seek first the God's kingdom 'and the things you need will be provided for you as well'.

DAY 2

Cleaning and polishing

The clearing is the start but not the whole job. Cleaning and polishing freshens the air, fragrance filling the room. The light lifts as surfaces gleam and reflect. It's tempting just to spray the polish into the air, but it never has quite the same effect somehow.

It's only when we have cleared the floor and surfaces that we can see how much it all needs a thorough clean and polish. You clear the ornaments off the sideboard and they leave those telltale circles of polished wood in a layer of dust! Well, mine do, anyway. Interesting, that. It reminds me of what Jesus said about a soul which has been cleared of evil spirits, leaving a highly desirable residence with no onward chain. And there's no shortage of dangerous, potential buyers.

Sometimes the clearing reveals a deep-seated and urgent structural problem – like the time I cleared an under-stair cupboard of junk and discovered a patch of damp plaster lurking at the bottom of it. That meant replacing an outdated damp course which was quite an upheaval, but I was so thankful I had found it before it got any worse. We may find that the extent and urgency of the cleaning and polishing required surprises us.

As you do any cleaning and polishing this week, think of your soul also getting a bit of maintenance and thorough cleaning. The kind of 'pulling out the piano and vacuuming behind the shoe rack' level of attention. This level of cleaning makes us sweat a bit and use our muscles, so we probably expect similar exertion requirements in the spiritual dimension as well. We often get into the habit of seeing sin as things we do, more than things we fail to do, so, for a change, work at getting in touch with the sin of not doing, of neglecting important spiritual areas and wasting your God-given experience of life as a result.

If you were to be looking around your soul as if it were a home, what areas might you find which had become covered with a layer of dust, for instance? Suppose that's your regular prayer time or daily Bible reading sitting there neglected. Or your thankful, praising heart, covered in cobwebs from long disuse. Or your thoughtfulness and generosity to others, or your humility. Imagine looking around the rooms of your soul and you'll find that as you 'see' the dust and cobwebs, you'll sense what it is that has been suffering from neglect, and it may make you feel sad or full of regret as you sense that your neglect has let yourself down, as well as God and the other people involved in your life.

Now look around the rooms of your soul and notice the cleaning, polishing and repairs which need doing because of stupid mistakes, thoughtless actions, accusing or destructive attitudes and behaviour, deliberate spoiling of relationships or events – those kinds of things. Imagine the pitted and scratched furniture and recognise where the blame actually lies with you and no one else. Notice the hurt you have caused by your actions and feel the sorrow that these things have happened.

Part of the putting right is acknowledging the problems without making your usual excuses to yourself. Don't be afraid to be honest with God for two reasons: first, God already knows your ways and your habits and what you are really like, and, second, God is still there looking lovingly at you with perhaps a smile beginning at the silly situation of you pretending where there isn't any need to be defensive at all.

Once you're acknowledging and recognising the problem, you will find welling up in you a passionate wish that it had been different, regret for time and opportunities wasted and the longing to be forgiven and set free. So go ahead and tell God how you feel. Tell him about your sadness and sorrow, and your longing for a fresh start. The technical word for the turmoil in you at the moment is repentance, and the twin sister of honest repentance is God's forgiveness.

What you need to do now is allow yourself to hear the free and tender forgiveness which the authentic God is assuring you of.

With God there is mercy and forgiveness (Psalm 116) and you can enjoy it to the full.

I wonder if you have ever tried to get rid of a stain and nothing seems to work? Sometimes it can feel like that spiritually as well. We come to God with our apology and request for forgiveness, know that God has forgiven us and then go back to thrashing ourselves with nettles and finding it impossible to get rid of the guilt.

There are plenty of reasons for this, and it's no good me saying, 'Well, you've got to trust that God has forgiven you and don't let yourself think those negative thoughts', because that will just make you feel a whole lot worse. You're now feeling guilty about feeling guilty!

Let's try thinking of it in a different way. Here you are with your spiritual marigolds on, scrubbing away at a stain that won't budge. Now imagine that Jesus comes along and gives you a completely new product, and asks you to let him use it on your problem area. Hand over the cloth and watch as Jesus uses the product and the stain dissolves completely away. It vanishes, with the surface restored just as if there never was a stain. It's even got rid of the damage caused by you scrubbing at it.

Now every time you get the worry that you are not forgiven, or that you are beyond forgiveness in this or that particular area, go through that exercise again. You see, the important thing to do is watch Jesus doing the work, not you. It will help wean you from this heavy sense of responsibility which blocks you from basking in God's unconditional love for you. The forgiving is not yours to do, but God's beautiful, effective product, called grace. Freely given and completely sufficient.

DAY 3

Creating the right atmosphere

If I asked you to think of a place anywhere in the world which always makes you feel uplifted, happy and at peace, I wonder where your mind would be taking you? Perhaps a place full of special memories, or somewhere which is particularly beautiful. Perhaps somewhere in which you feel you can be comfortably yourself.

It's not always possible to put your finger on what precisely gives a place a particular atmosphere, but lots of people pick up on houses that have a good feel to them, and animals are even more sensitive to the feel of a place, relaxing or going on the defensive instinctively.

When we decorate the house for Christmas it's a particular atmosphere we are trying to create. We want the house to feel festive and magical, full of the Christmas spirit of warmth, welcome and hospitality. Perhaps we want a sense of the traditional, with a hint of Christmases our grandparents and great-grandparents celebrated. Perhaps we want there to be style and glamour, with a sense of luxury and opulence. Maybe it's an atmosphere of fun and excitement we're after.

This Advent, as we prepare our decorations for Christmas, we're going to be thinking about creating the right atmosphere in our hearts as well as our homes. An atmosphere which reflects the real meaning of Christmas and best provides an environment for the Christmas message to take root and flourish in us.

So what are our celebrations all about? What makes it worth our while investing so much time and energy on decorating our homes and places of work and town centres at this season of the year? New babies are mostly a good reason for celebrating, and there's a baby at the heart of Christmas. It must be to do with who that baby is. A baby considered so important for so many that the very date is now counted from his birth.

That's an extraordinary decision to make. For the event to have had such impact on international thinking, there must be something completely extraordinary about this baby. It suggests that as a result of his birth nothing was ever going to be quite the same again.

And that is what Christians are saying by putting up the decorations both in their homes and in their hearts. It's a huge collaborative 'Thank you!' to God, that at a particular moment in history God entered our human world as a human baby so as to show himself to us in the only language we can really understand – the human language, the language of a human life lived out in total love and forgiveness, wherever that might lead.

It's an incredulous sense of utter wonder and amazement at the extent of God's love for us. It's a bubbling up of relief and joy that, in spite of everything, there really is hope for us and eternal meaning to our mortal lives. It's a realisation that the heavenly, so often hidden from our physical sight, is only just beyond our vision, and is always breaking in on the earthly in a holy, mysterious and beautiful way. It speaks to us not only of what God is really like but also of what we are really like, and what we might become if we can touch base with this level of reality.

No wonder we celebrate and decorate our homes. No wonder it is worth preparing our hearts as well, to celebrate in style.

As you plan your decorating, put the Christchild back into the very centre of the atmosphere you create. Think about the kind of crib you have and where you place it. Let all the other decorations draw their shout of thanks and praise and wonder and joy from that. Create an atmosphere of the heavenly breaking into the earthly, the love and humility, the holiness and the deepest, truest magic of all.

And at the same time deck out your heart and soul as a place made ready and welcoming for Christ in the deep centre of your being. You will need to clear a space of time to prepare for the celebration of Christmas, and the decision to do so will actually be part of the preparations. The truth is that we always make time for what we consider the highest priorities, so it's more a question of shifting priorities than carving out time – to find time, something else will have to be thought of as less important, and that can be a hard decision to make.

Find somewhere, even for a short while, where you are able to be relaxed and attentive to God's prompting. That may be while you walk along, over an early-morning mug of tea or coffee, on the train or in the bath. You may like to go into church or the local library. Could you swap childcare with someone at your church for an hour so you can both do this quiet preparation in turn?

In the quietness, think over or read again the Christmas narratives in Matthew, Luke or the prologue of John's gospel. Imagine Mary's and Joseph's heart and how they were able to accept that new future with a profound 'Yes'. Then imagine yourself creating a place of welcome and openness to God by working on your heart and soul.

Slowly and carefully in your heart, prepare garlands of love and thankfulness, wide spaces of expectant listening, a cave of humility, clean cloths and fresh straw of practical caring service. Place lamps of hope and patience to shine bright in the darkness, and hang stars of faith and trust in the sky.

DAY 4

Lighting dark corners

Most high street shopping areas have their Christmas lighting-up parties, and suddenly there are snowmen and stars and snowflakes reflected in the wet tarmac, so that everyone feels more Christmassy and hopefully does more shopping and spends more money. And every year more homes and streets join in the illuminations game, with lit-up reindeer shining on the roofs, Santas waving out of chimneys, icicle lights trickling from the eaves and window frames marked out by flashing colours.

We celebrate Christmas in the northern hemisphere at a very dark, cold time of year, with plenty of night during normal waking hours, so the darkness makes a perfect backdrop for illuminated decorations. It's one way of tackling the winter gloom to turn the darkness into an art studio and play with it. It cheers us up and helps us enjoy what we would otherwise find very depressing.

It's not that the dark days of winter are wrong, of course. They're just a natural part of living on a round planet home which orbits a star. There are bound to be periods of darkness and light on a daily and yearly cycle. And this is also true of our lives and the human condition. The myth of the moment is that everyone else's normal is a state of constant sunshine – highest pleasure and happiness with everything going right for them. The truth is that normal for all of us is actually a wave with peaks and troughs of ecstatic and depressing times and most of life running somewhere through the middle.

Unfortunately, the myth feeds us with a false, unsustainable expectation that the normal we ought to be experiencing floats lightly along, brushing pleasantly against those highest peaks, and that anything different is somehow inferior. This leaves us in a semi-permanent state of disappointment and resentment.

Well, suppose we readjust our thinking, in two ways. First, we recognise and accept that real life is supposed to be a pattern of light and darkness – that's part of the design. And, second, we start using any darkness as a backdrop to play with light: God's light.

The places of darkness we live through are as valid and as useful to us as the brightest times. Sometimes they turn out to be the very places where we learn most and grow as people. Often those who seem to have a lovely healing compassion, with wisdom and gentleness or a thankfulness which is infectious, turn out to be those who have been through some really difficult and challenging experiences, rather than those who have always been indulged and had no opportunities to practise the skills of unselfishness. So look at the darker patches through a new pair of glasses and start noticing the difference.

I remember the day I first decided to do this, after reading *The Cloud of Unknowing*. We had travelled for six hours with two children under five and were staying at a bed and breakfast before a friend's wedding the next day. Both children threw up one after the other all night long! It was a brilliant chance to try out my new way of looking at the darker patches of life. And I was amazed by the difference it made.

I found I was able to use the situation as practice in coping graciously with disappointment and frustration, and finding blessings within the messy and less than perfect situation (a nearby bin had come in handy, and the girls seemed to be taking turns rather than both together, for instance, and yes, there was a toilet and running water in the same building). I found I seemed to have more resources of compassion and patience and perseverance than I normally would have, and can only think that in doing it God's way I was accessing God's resources.

I certainly found a very odd thing happening – as the night wore on, I was thanking and praising God quite genuinely and not through gritted teeth, accepting cheerfully what I normally would have felt sore about. So for me it was a minor miracle, and I can recommend it for suddenly opening up a life which is happier and with fewer tensions, altogether more contented and at peace.

Although since that night all those years ago I have been through far darker and more challenging places, I have found it always works, and I agree with David the king and psalm writer when he wrote, 'Yes, even though I walk through the darkest valley – the valley of the shadow of death – I fear no evil, for you are with me; your rod and your staff give me comfort.'

David must have discovered what I and millions of others have found true: that God is light in our places of darkness, and once we start working within that, rather than manically stamping our feet and trying to cheat the system, all the bright light of God is at our disposal and we understand a little more that God's values don't always match up with ours, and nothing is ever wasted with God. No experience, however dark, is ever wasted, because God transforms it with light.

DAY 5

Dressing the tree

Christmas trees became popular in England after Queen Victoria's husband Albert introduced the tradition from Germany. The evergreen of the pine or spruce tree was a symbol of God's everlasting love; the baubles were fruits of the spirit – love, joy, peace, patience, kindness, goodness, gentleness and self-control (Galatians 5:22); and the little candle lights which used to be fixed to the branches were reminders that Jesus is the Light of the World. At the very top of the tree there would be either an angel or a star. Any other sparkly decorations would reflect the light as we can reflect God's love. The Christmas tree was like a tree of life, with everyone's wrapped gifts underneath its branches, proclaiming Jesus, the greatest gift of all.

Well, there have been changes to some of those traditions, of course, sometimes for the sake of practical good sense. Having a tree full of resin lit up by candles was not exactly the safest of ideas, especially in a room full of children and excitement but strings of electrically powered lights do the same kind of job. And many of us can't stand the inconvenience of dropped needles so opt for a plastic version, or one which keeps the shape but experiments with glowing or sparkling branches.

Even now, though, many people still prefer the good smell of a fresh pine or spruce tree, and often the whole family is involved in the decorating, so that some of the decorations are of the gluey and carefully hand-cut variety. I still have some of those that the grandchildren make with such care.

It used to add to the Christmas magic in many homes that the Christmas tree would be decorated only after the children had gone to bed on Christmas Eve, so that the living room was completely transformed on Christmas morning. At the moment we're going through a phase of getting the tree in position as one of the first signs of Christmas coming. That's exciting, but has the downside of having to calm the rising tide of anticipation in little ones who can hardly bear the suspense when it's so drawn out, particularly with all those intriguing parcels you're never allowed to tear open.

Well, what about this year? How can we take a fresh look at our Christmas tree and start using it again as a sign to help us all reflect on the meaning of Christmas while we get ready for the special day?

In the light of the evergreen symbol you might reconsider having an evergreen tree, however little, so that every time you catch sight of it, green in the middle of winter, it reminds you of God's evergreen love. Even if you haven't got the real thing, any Christmas tree can be a reminder, though. God is never fickle. He doesn't just keep our plates spinning, giving each of us a brief bit of attention during a crisis and then ignoring us until we cry out in desperation again. His eye is always on us, watching and loving us, feeling for us in our pain and rejoicing with us in our joy.

There are no frozen places of dark winter in our lives where the leaves of God's love fall off. Whatever time of life we are at, and whatever we are going through, God's love stays fresh, green and steadfast. As the hymn puts it, 'New every morning is the love our waking and uprising prove.' We are living proof of God's evergreen love, because if God forgot about us or stopped loving us, there would be no waking and uprising.

Our mortal span of living as humans on planet earth is a priceless gift and an expression of God's love that goes on and on through all the generations of people. Seeing it like that will alter our perception of how we are to use our life and our attitude to those with whom we share our section of living.

And what about those baubles and other tree decorations? Let's look again at what Paul identified as fruits of a life rooted in God's Spirit: love, joy, peace, patience, kindness, goodness, gentleness and self-control. As you hang the decorations on your tree of evergreen love, keep that list handy, or even memorise it. Or make each of them into tree decorations so that you can physically see the spiritual truth of them. (Cross stitch would work, or sticking transfer letters on to baubles, or cutting the words out of hologram card, punching a hole and threading with thin silver or gold string.)

Pray for God to equip you with whatever you need to be a spiritually fruiting tree, fragrant and a blessing to the people you meet and the situation in which you dwell. Leave the actual fruits up to God. Jesus explained that the fruiting will happen naturally and automatically if we make sure we are good trees, rooted in God's life and love. 'Make a tree good and its fruit will be good' (Matthew 12:33, NIV). And thank God, as you hang those Christmas tree 'fruits' of baubles and chocolate, for the fruiting you can see in the lives of other people – those around you and also good lives you might be struck by in a brief interview on the news or in a documentary.

Then the Christmas tree lights. As you drape them around your tree, think of dressing your own life in the light of Jesus, so that your life shines with his love and truth and goodness. Allow Jesus the permission to do that shining in you, rather than trying to do it for yourself. And if you find he's answering your prayer by giving you some stretching practice, take in good heart and be thankful for the opportunity to learn.

DAY 6

Sparkle

The reason we use lots of sparkle in our decorations at Christmas is to do with its clever reflecting skill. It magnifies any light source and plays around with it, throwing it from one surface to another. We've probably all played that reflecting game with a shiny object and the sun at school, directing the reflected light on someone's face and watching the effect.

And we see it powerfully in the brightness of the moon, lit by the reflected light of the sun so brightly sometimes that we can see our shadows at night. Chandeliers used the reflection method to add power to candlelight, bouncing the light off the different surfaces of glass beads to make the whole hanging filled with light.

I suppose I could have called this Advent book 'Sparkle' because we are working at reflection on the Christmas light in all the different kinds of surfaces, shapes and colours of our Christmas preparation. And you could say that as Christians we are commissioned to be pieces of tinsel. That sounds quite an odd commissioning, doesn't it, and not particularly noble, really. Christmas trees, perhaps, but surely not just mundane, homely tinsel!

Let's think again. When Paul and his companions came to start a gathering of the church at the Roman town of Philippi, the capital town of Macedonia, they went outside the city gates, by the river. Sure enough, as they had expected, there were some people gathering out there to pray. And they were women. Women, outside the security of the gates of the city. And they were the ones Paul found offering a house for the church to meet in.

Or what about that story Jesus told of the traveller mugged between Jerusalem and Jericho. Who was it reflected God's light by reaching out to a fellow human being in great need? One of those unmentionables for orthodox Jews at the time – a Samaritan man. It would be like saying a Palestinian today.

Jesus often drew attention to the value of doing the little acts of kindness beautifully, and that's what Mother Theresa picked up on and dedicated her life to. At the beginning she was laughed at for the paucity of the help she was able to give by gathering in a few abandoned babies in the huge terrible, overwhelming poverty of India. But she pressed on, convinced that although we may each be unable to do a great deal, we can all do something beautiful for God. The example of Mother Teresa and others like her inspires people and refreshes their spirit.

Perhaps we are a bit like tinsel and no grander than that. But a humble spirit, which does its valiant shining even if it isn't highly regarded, and isn't built to last, and sometimes gets tangled up and drops bits which someone has to clean up after, is precious in God's sight and greatly regarded.

In Psalm 103 it says, 'As a father has compassion on his children, so the Lord has compassion on those who fear him; for he knows how we are formed, he remembers that we are dust.' The lovely thing about God is that we never have to try and be what we aren't. God really does understand that we aren't always the great shiny reflecting mirrors or chandeliers which do a near perfect job of reflecting his love in shining lives.

But if we are just homely tinsel, God will still give us the important, urgent reflecting work to do, rather as we encourage our toddlers to help with the gardening or dusting. Much more than the actual extent of their skill, what touches us is their conscientious keenness to join in and help. Well, God's the same with us. He loves seeing us working at our shining lives of loving service and forgiveness. He doesn't chuck us out because we are still learning, or are a bit broken in places. Every bit of reflective shining brightens the light of God's love in the world.

Mary realised that when she found she of all people had been chosen to be the mother of God's Son. Her own ordinariness was not an obstacle to God at all. In fact, he seems to have treasured it. 'He has chosen to lift up the humble rather than choose the powerful,' Mary sings in amazement, and that's typical of a God who is prepared to humble himself, lay aside his majesty and share our human nature, just so that he can save us through loving us completely where we are.

Essentially, what causes a sparkle is when a suitable surface faces the light. So that must be our job to work on as we take the opportunity to watch any sparkling in our decorations around the house or town today. Let's turn our faces to the light of Jesus' amazing love, and as we look at it there it will start doing its shining work in us. People may notice that we look more relaxed and happy, that our eyes are softer and more interested as we listen properly to what other people are saying to us. They may notice that we don't seem to be as critical as usual, or moody, or negative. What has happened?

We may be only tinsel, but God is making us sparkle!

DAY 7

Something to think, something to pray and something to do

Something to think . . .

Think back over the process of clearing, cleaning and polishing, creating the right atmosphere, lighting dark corners, dressing the tree and sparkling. And make good use of all those symbols of God's love, which are all around you everywhere at the moment.

Something to pray . . .

Lord God, thank you for healing me
with the blessing of your forgiveness.
Thank you for your generous, shining love
that changes crusted lives and broken spirits.
Thank you that you love us as we are
and are happy to enlist our help
in the lighting of dark places,
bringing hope and joy.
Blessed be God for ever.
Amen.

Something to do . . .

1 Polish a surface until it gleams.

2 Be kind to someone who needs your help.

3 Let a toddler, or someone elderly, frail or slow, help you in a job so that you learn the beauty of God's agenda.

WEEK 3

CAROL SINGING

DAY 1

O come, O come, Emmanuel

1 O come, O come, Emmanuel,
and ransom captive Israel,
that mourns in lonely exile here,
until the Son of God appear.

Rejoice, rejoice!
Emmanuel shall come to thee,
O Israel.

2 O come, thou rod of Jesse, free
thine own from Satan's tyranny;
from depths of hell thy people save,
and give them victory o'er the grave.

3 O come, thou dayspring, come and cheer
our spirits by thine advent here;
disperse the gloomy clouds of night,
and death's dark shadows put to flight.

4 O come, thou key of David, come
and open wide our heavenly home;
make safe the way that leads on high,
and close the path to misery.

5 O come, O come, thou Lord of might,
who to thy tribes on Sinai's height
in ancient times didst give the Law,
in cloud and majesty and awe.

Translated from the 'Great O Antiphons' (12th–13th century)
by John Mason Neale (1818–1866)

This is usually the time of many carol services. Some of us are involved in several of them and may have relatives singing, reading or performing in them. Or we may be the ones preparing the service or concert, among the colds and coughs.

I thought it might be useful to you if this week we took a different carol each day and thought about it, so that when you are practising or listening to those familiar words you can click off the auto-pilot and feel the freshness once again.

So today's carol is a gasp of longing, a traditional Advent carol, which puts us in touch with the years of waiting and hoping over many generations: 'O come, O come, Emmanuel!'

All the longing and hoping of the verses is counterbalanced by joyful trust in the promise of the chorus: 'Rejoice, rejoice! Emmanuel *shall* come to thee, O Israel.' There is a light and shadow, question and answer, gloom and affirmation contrast as we take a walk in empathy through the pages of Jewish history and prophecy.

You know those interminable journeys that sometimes happen, often late at night, when the train service is disrupted and everyone piles out into a bus between several stations. And then the elderly bus breaks down so everyone gets out and shivers in the wind while another vehicle is allocated. And then you miss your connection and have an hour's wait on the cold echoing platform where you can't buy a hot drink. *Those* kind of journeys!

That's what it must have felt like in a 'whole nation and many generations' scale for the people of Israel as they wandered in the wilderness for forty years after escaping from slavery in Egypt on dry land through the Red Sea, and as they wandered spiritually when they were exiled as a people many years later. It must feel as if the journey was never going to end.

We probably all know those times when there is no option but to stick your helmet on and make the most of a grim situation. There is a real sense of deep weariness in the middle of the determination to keep going, and what keeps them going is the strong conviction that God, who had rescued them from Egypt and given them the Law at Sinai, was indeed going to accomplish the greatest rescue of all for the whole world.

And somehow they were going to be instrumental in making that possible. Their calling was to be a holy people, a light to the nations as they kept hope alive and waited for God to act.

The prophets were there, sometimes shaking the people to get their lives in better shape, and sometimes recognising that there was a special relationship between God and his people, so that God goes on loving and forgiving and drawing them back to the code of love, however much they mess things up. Giving up is not what God is about.

We know from the gospels that God did indeed keep his promise to be Emmanuel – God with us – and to make the ultimate rescue possible from our own sin and evil, that most dangerous and poisonous form of slavery. God keeps his promise so that not only the Jewish people but the citizenship of the whole world may benefit from that work of rescue.

So when you hear or sing this hymn this Advent, use it with its haunting melody and longing words to stand with all those who feel that their whole life is a waiting to be rescued from loneliness, pain or oppression, fear, guilt or some kind of exile. Let the strong conviction and hope of the chorus become God's blessing of promise and his reassurance to accompany them in their suffering every step of the way.

Feel yourself part of the great long story of God's rescue – from Abraham, Isaac, Jacob and Joseph, through Moses and Joshua, Saul, David and all the kings, to the splitting of the northern and southern parts of the kingdom, the exile, and the return that isn't quite the fulfilment longed for.

Sense God's humility and love and mercy in the way he stays with us through the times we get it wrong or misunderstand, and uses spokespeople who are prepared to brave rejection for speaking out what many do not want to hear. Sense that bright, strong thread of hope which we can all trust in the parts of our own life journey which are painful, lonely or arduous. And be freshly surprised by the way the God of Sinai comes to his people as Emmanuel: little and dependent, as vulnerable as Adam.

DAY 2

O little town of Bethlehem

1 O little town of Bethlehem,
how still we see thee lie!
Above thy deep and dreamless sleep
the silent stars go by.
Yet in thy dark streets shineth
the everlasting light;
the hopes and fears of all the years
are met in thee tonight.

2 O morning stars, together
proclaim the holy birth,
and praises sing to God the King,
and peace to all the earth.
For Christ is born of Mary;
and, gathered all above,
while mortals sleep, the angels keep
their watch of wondering love.

3 How silently, how silently,
the wondrous gift is given!
So God imparts to human hearts
the blessings of his heaven.
No ear may hear his coming;
but in this world of sin,
where meek souls will receive him still,
the dear Christ enters in.

4 O holy child of Bethlehem,
descend to us, we pray;
cast out our sin and enter in,
be born in us today.

We hear the Christmas angels
the great glad tidings tell:
O come to us, abide with us,
our Lord Emmanuel.

Phillips Brooks (1835–1893)

Today's carol draws the heavenly and the earthly together so that we are helped to see both at once. We keep being shown the vast universe and then hurtled into the immediacy and intimacy of the little family in a corner of the town. Just look at the contrast and paradox in that first verse of the sky filled with stars and yet the everlasting light nestling in the dark streets of Bethlehem. God, Phillips Brooks is saying, is both transcendent and also immanent, both all-powerful and also concerned with us in a face-to-face encounter.

Every so often I get an urge to go travelling to somewhere exotic, and I enjoy experiencing different cultures and ways of thinking. But when I'm there, wherever 'there' happens to be, one of the things I enjoy most is that, for the people living here, this is their local and ordinary, and mine is the exotic. Wherever you travel it will be someone's local neighbourhood and not exotic at all!

This carol marvels at the way the God of earth and heaven can be born down a local street where people snooze and snore even though this extraordinary event has just happened. Yet that is actually the profound truth about the Incarnation, that God did not choose to come with any special privileges or bodyguards, like a prince at university.

Hardly anybody even knew about it. Phillips Brooks marvels again at the lack of fanfare. 'How silently the wondrous gift is given.' And isn't that exactly the way God makes himself known to us usually – it's when we are ready to be still and wait in reverence and humility that we sense the presence of God.

All the stars of heaven, spreading out from the whole of the universe to this place above Bethlehem, express the splendour of God's glory. All the hopes and fears of all the years have been leading to this moment and stretch away from it, out to our own times and the moment you are singing or hearing those words.

We hover in this most precious and holy moment of stillness, where heaven becomes grounded in the local nature of human life so that at the same time it becomes possible for our humanness to access the glory of heaven. A beautiful two-way exchange and embrace.

Suddenly we each of us can become that local place where God comes to dwell in humility, gracing us with his presence and quietly making himself known in the deep heart of us.

And out of that full, compassionate heart will come our aching prayer for the healing of the town of Bethlehem, surrounded as it is at present by the huge barrier of the security fence, its inhabitants shut off from relatives and friends who live outside and with only one checkpoint in and out of the city.

Christians living in Bethlehem with whom I have talked do find it hard to understand the silence of Christians around the world, and the lack of support and encouragement from them. We need to keep in touch with our brothers and sisters there and encourage them with our love and prayers.

More of us need to make a point of visiting Bethlehem and staying in people's homes there, so as to understand something of what they are going through. We need to experience with them the long queues at the checkpoint and observe the treatment they are getting. We need to hear their stories of pain and frustration, their hopes and their fears. Instead of swallowing the propaganda stories about security risks to tourists there, we need to put our faith into action and simply go. There is nothing like a Bethlehem welcome and Bethlehem hospitality.

Going in person is the best sign to anyone in pain that you really care. Perhaps out of this Advent will grow the possibility of more friendship visits and a more responsible understanding of what it means to be members of the whole Body of Christ.

DAY 3

It came upon the midnight clear

1 It came upon the midnight clear,
that glorious song of old,
from angels bending near the earth
to touch their harps of gold:
'Peace on the earth, goodwill to all,
from heaven's all-gracious King!'
The world in solemn stillness lay
to hear the angels sing.

2 Still through the cloven skies they come,
with peaceful wings unfurled;
and still their heavenly music floats
o'er all the weary world;
above its sad and lowly plains
they bend on hovering wing;
and ever o'er its Babel-sounds
the blessed angels sing.

3 Yet with the woes of sin and strife
the world has suffered long;
beneath the angel-strain have rolled
two thousand years of wrong;
and warring humankind hears not
the love-song which they bring;
O hush the noise of mortal strife,
and hear the angels sing!

4 And ye, beneath life's crushing load,
whose forms are bending low,
who toil along the climbing way
with painful steps and slow:

look now! for glad and golden hours
come swiftly on the wing;
O rest beside the weary road,
and hear the angels sing.

5 For lo, the days are hastening on,
by prophets seen of old,
when with the ever-circling years
comes round the age of gold;
when peace shall over all the earth
its ancient splendours fling,
and all the world give back the song
which now the angels sing.

Edmund Sears (1810-1876)

This carol talks about holy listening. Listening skills are taught in our nursery and infant schools, and I like the way children get training in all the things that get us ready for good listening, like sitting still, making eye contact, taking turns with speaking and so on. The little ones will perhaps have photos taken of them showing good listening, and all this helps them to be better aware of listening as a purposeful activity which we have to practise and commit ourselves to.

Well, I reckon we adults need some of that training too. So often we end up both talking together, or playing subtle control games with one another in the way we interrupt, or we spend the listening time in a conversation planning what we are going to say next instead of giving our undivided attention to the present speaker.

We need to reawaken our listening skills in our households and places of work as well. Christians ought to be famous for their excellent listening, because the way we listen to each other emerges from the way we listen to God in prayer. Every conversation we have with any other person is holy ground; a place where 'Love your neighbour as yourself' is bedrock.

Edmund Sears is clearly feeling deafened by the raucous noise of aggressive strife in the world of his time, and he contrasts that with the quiet peace of the angels' song. It's like Elijah hearing the 'still small voice' as he stands at the cave entrance after the strong wind and the fire.

Every lifetime and every generation has its clamour and strife which blocks out the angels' song. The heavenly message of peace and joy can only be heard properly when we learn to be still and attentive, open to hear it. Often we deliberately drown it out so it can't be heard. Now why on earth would we do that? Surely a love song from heaven is attractive, and you'd expect everyone to be tuning in to it all the time.

Well, yes, it certainly is beautiful and fulfilling, but what puts us off wanting to hear it is that it creates a discord with everything selfish, power-hungry, false and wrong. That's the problem for us: either we must decide to put down any of those agendas and hear the song of heaven properly, or, if we really don't want to stop pleasing ourselves at all costs, we shall have to drown out that music so it can't challenge us and make us feel uncomfortable about the way we are living.

There are times when it would be so convenient to cover God's eyes while we rage and criticise, or act unfaithfully, or break a promise or cheat. These are the real battles – the war in us of how we exercise our gift of free will. This is the battlefield Jesus was talking about when he said, 'If anyone keeps trying to save his life, he will end up losing it, but anyone who is prepared to lose his life for me will save it' (Luke 9:24).

The odd thing is that the grace and courage to live heaven's way comes from hearing heaven's song in our hearts. The more we hear it, the more attractive it becomes, so that the cost of it – living with God at the centre instead of self – becomes more and more worth spending, and that is what empowers us in those daily battles.

The alternative to God's way fades into rubbish beside the rich beauty of living in the company and service of the God of earth and heaven. As Paul found himself declaring, 'I consider everything garbage, compared to the surpassing greatness of knowing Christ Jesus my Lord, for whose sake I have lost all things' (Philippians 3:8).

So if we catch the merest whisper of God's song of love, it's well worth putting our listening skills into practice and settling ourselves to hear it properly. Put aside time to be still in God's presence. Or sing through this carol, or your favourite verse of it, while you are doing other things today, reminding yourself that this love song was the song your life was created to sing. One day, the whole world will give back the song which now the angels sing. And you will be part of that, singing your heart out and full of heaven's joy.

DAY 4

Away in a manger

1 Away in a manger,
no crib for a bed,
the little Lord Jesus
laid down his sweet head.
The stars in the bright sky
looked down where he lay,
the little Lord Jesus
asleep on the hay.

2 The cattle are lowing,
the baby awakes,
but little Lord Jesus
no crying he makes.
I love thee, Lord Jesus!
Look down from the sky,
and stay by my side
until morning is nigh.

or *The cattle are lowing,*
they also adore
the little Lord Jesus
who lies in the straw.
I love you, Lord Jesus,
I know you are near
to love and protect me
till morning is here.

3 Be near me, Lord Jesus,
I ask thee to stay
close by me for ever
and love me I pray.
Bless all the dear children
in thy tender care,
and fit us for heaven
to live with thee there.

William Kirkpatrick (1838–1921);
alternative text verse 2 by Michael Forster (b. 1946)

This is probably the first carol we all learn, isn't it, and, with every new generation, tears are brought to the eyes of adults hearing the words sung by very young voices. I'm sure you will be hearing it sung at some point this week!

At last year's crib service on Christmas Eve, Mary was played by a two-year-old who I found absorbed in playing her part before the service, kneeling quietly by the manger in the straw and stroking the Jesus doll as she sang her version of this carol to him. It was a moment of holy ground again, to come across reverent worship like that, so simple and natural.

I've often found toddlers worship easily in the context of the Christmas crib. One Christmas I found a two-year-old boy piling hay on to the baby in the manger. 'Jesus looks cold', he explained when I came up. That's worship.

We can learn so much from the very young, humbling as that may be, because sometimes we assume we adults are the ones who really know, and have a duty to teach the little ones. I'm not so sure. I think we'd do better to learn from them things like worshipping naturally, with wonder and curiosity at anything and everything, not pretending to be anything other than ourselves, knowing when we don't know and knowing that we have needs.

It is an extraordinary and holy marvel that God entered our world as a baby. Babies and toddlers are messy, demanding and noisy, and as you watch them grow and develop their characters, it's like seeing the human story unfolding freshly in each one. I've included an alternative version of verse 2 by Michael Forster because of this. It rather bothers me that in William Kirkpatrick's original version – coming from the Victorian culture, of course – there is a hint of Jesus not doing the ordinary baby things like crying when he wakes up. I would hate us to get the impression that some of the noisier, messier aspects of babyhood are not part of the Incarnation.

In fact, I am sure the opposite is true – God in Jesus was taking on the full package of human nature, even with the screams and tantrums of the two-year-old and the crying of the baby waking up and needing milk or a change of swaddling clothes. Mary was a real mother, both cuddling and cross sometimes, and no doubt sharp with Jesus when he was crawling dangerously around the furniture and Joseph's carpentry tools, and when his strength of character was developing.

I love the truth that Jesus was in a real family and had brothers and sisters, grandparents and cousins, and there must have been arguments as well as fun, just like in every family. That's why we can talk everything over with Jesus, our brother, and know he understands our human condition. He's been there and got the T-shirt.

This carol gives us a glimpse of Jesus as a vulnerable and innocent baby, completely approachable because of that. I often think how convenient it is that an older sister or brother has several months of the new baby being very little and sweet and unable to move much before the crawling and 'joining in' stage. It gives us space to build affection so that we're a bit better able to cope with that when it happens!

Lots of people enjoy looking at new babies and we are drawn to love them and engage with them. How beautiful that God comes to us first as a baby, then. Perhaps that's why Christmas is still a time when people are comfortable to come into our churches and worship. The innocence of a new baby works its deep magic on us, awaking in us the sense of wonder and a whisper of who we really are. Children of God, born of God's love and known by name. 'Trailing clouds of glory', as Wordsworth put it.

As you hear or sing this carol, the most popular one of all, and as you see any young baby, thank God for his amazing humility and understanding of our humanness. As Julian of Norwich saw, 'he upholds us in compassion and pity, as if we were children, innocent and eager.'

DAY 5

In the bleak mid-winter

1 In the bleak mid-winter
frosty wind made moan,
earth stood hard as iron,
water like a stone;
snow had fallen, snow on snow,
snow on snow,
in the bleak mid-winter, long ago.

2 Our God, heaven cannot hold him
nor earth sustain;
heaven and earth shall flee away
when he comes to reign.
In the bleak mid-winter
a stable-place sufficed
the Lord God almighty, Jesus Christ.

3 Enough for him, whom cherubim
worship night and day,
a breastful of milk,
and a mangerful of hay:
enough for him, whom angels
fall down before,
the ox and ass and camel which adore.

4 Angels and archangels
may have gathered there,
cherubim and seraphim
thronged the air;
but only his mother
in her maiden bliss
worshiped the belovèd with a kiss.

5 What can I give him,
poor as I am?
If I were a shepherd
I would bring a lamb;
if I were a wise man
I would do my part,
yet what I can I give him: give my heart.

Christina Rossetti (1830–1894)

This well-loved and tender carol is poetry at its best, able to touch our hearts with a word and set off in us a deep sense of love which makes us glad to be human. I think it is all about God's love and our response to it.

That's why Christina Rossetti spends the whole of the first verse creating for us a picture of an earth which is hard, icy and frozen under layers of snow. We pick up on the bleak, unresponsive, unwelcoming cold of Narnia where it was 'always winter but never Christmas', and of those bleak words in the prologue of John's gospel: 'He came unto his own but his own received him not.'

There is the sense of a build-up of hardened hearts and attitudes, over years in individual lives and collectively in generations, including ours, and we are not allowed to pass over it quickly. Rossetti wants the cold and hardness to establish its presence in us so that the rest of the poem will work more powerfully.

In the second verse she moves completely away from the cold, frozen earth, to describe God in all his glory and power and majesty, whom heaven cannot hold nor earth sustain. So powerful is this God that the whole of earth and heaven will melt away when he comes to reign. Then, suddenly, we are brought back to the bleak, mid-winter earth, unwelcoming to its maker, and yet a welcome is given by an ordinary stable, and that is both enough and plenty for almighty God in the miracle of littleness. God lays all that vast power and glory aside to be born as Jesus, the Christ, the anointed One. The earth has given the welcome it can: a stable-place.

Now Rossetti ponders the enormity of what is happening. You can't get more majestic than having angelic cherubim giving unceasing worship, day and night throughout eternity. Yet the wonder of it is that God is content with the gifts that earth can give – human mothering and feeding, the warmth of dried grass as a bed to sleep in, and animals acknowledging in their animal way that the baby in their stable is to be reverenced and protected.

Actually God is more than simply content. What Rossetti is suggesting is that these earthly and human responses of care and love are beautiful and precious to God, and we are privileged as humans to be able to give God what God most longs for: a relationship of love with our Creator. It is our worship as humans that completes God's great plan of creation, and in worship we become most fully our true human selves. This is exactly what we were created for 'in the image and likeness of God' (Genesis 1).

The next verse tracks that thought even deeper. Yes, there may well have been all the hosts of heaven, largely hidden from human eyes, crowding into the little stable-place, but now earth is the place of holiness, and the gift of a kiss from a human mother to her beloved son is like the highest act of worship any being could ever give. Through this birth, God has lifted humanity into a more intimate level with God than ever before. It is as if we are back in the Garden of Eden again, where there is warm, intimate relationship, affection and communication. Mary represents our loving human response as she worships the beloved with a kiss.

And so from Mary on to each of us. The thaw of that bleak midwinter has begun wherever a human heart is touched to respond to God in love. It is built in to our Godly nature to want to respond to love by giving. That is deep and beautiful in us. It is at the heart of the creation of new life, where a baby is born from two humans loving, responding and giving as they make love.

Immediately we respond to this love of God by asking ourselves, 'What can *I* give him, poor as I am?' Rossetti thinks over this. Well, the shepherd would be able to give a lamb, the wise man to do his part, so it follows that the only gift worth giving is the thing we are *able* to give. There is a lovely sense of gladness in suddenly realising what the gift needs to be and the happiness in choosing to give it. We give what we have, and as humans we have the highest privilege of a heart to offer God. It is with joy and love that we can sing, 'Yet what I have, I give him: give my heart!'

DAY 6

O come, all ye faithful

1 O come, all ye faithful,
joyful and triumphant,
O come ye, O come ye to Bethlehem;
come and behold him, born the king of angels:

O come, let us adore him,
O come, let us adore him,
O come, let us adore him,
Christ the Lord.

2 God of God,
Light of Light,
lo, he abhors not the Virgin's womb;
very God, begotten not created:

3 Child, for us sinners
poor and in the manger,
fain we embrace thee, with love and awe;
who would not love thee, loving us so dearly?

4 Sing, choirs of angels,
sing in exultation,
sing, all ye citizens of heaven above;
glory to God in the highest:

5 Yea, Lord, we greet thee,
born this happy morning,
Jesus, to thee be glory given;
Word of the Father, now in flesh appearing:

Attributed to John Francis Wade (1711–1786); translated by Frederick Oakeley (1802–1880) and others

When I was at school we always sang this carol in its original Latin. My Latin was never very good so I'm not sure how much I understood, but its grand solemnity has marked it out as being fitting for the final roof-lifting hymn of carol services everywhere. You feel rooted in theological scholarship and tradition, almost like singing a Credal faith statement. In fact, come to think of it, it would work quite well as this at any time of year, if you left out the particularly Christmassy final verse.

That was another rule – we were not allowed to sing that last verse apart from Christmas Day, so Midnight Mass and Christmas morning were the only time we sang it, and we sang it in English! I can remember a thrill of excitement at midnight when we sang out, 'Word of the Father, now in flesh appearing', and it was as if all the years between melted away and I was there in the stable witnessing the very act of Incarnation taking place.

I still love the 'now' word, and often when I pray, 'Glory to the Father, and to the Son, and to the Holy Spirit, as it was in the beginning, is now . . . and shall be for ever', I hang there in that 'now', conscious of God's vibrant presence within me, all around me and in every part of the universe. I find myself merging into God's presence and needing to be completely still in honour of a reality deeper than everything else. No words necessary, just God in the 'now' as I pray.

It is a bit like when you walk along and suddenly become aware of a rare bird or wild animal, and you keep still, hardly breathing and giving it your full attention before it moves away.

That whole line 'Word of the Father, now in flesh appearing' is linked with the prologue in the gospel of John: 'And the Word was made flesh and dwelt among us. And we beheld his glory, the glory as of the only begotten of the Father, full of grace and truth' (John 1:14, King James Authorised).

Here is God expressing himself. And the word of expression he uses is a human life, so that we humans will understand the language with no gap of communication. What we see in the gospel reports of Jesus expresses to us in the language of a human life the very nature and person of God.

We find Jesus in ongoing conversations with his disciples, and in regular, constant communication with his Father in heaven. We find him teaching and explaining to people in a way they can readily access, listening with humility, acting with compassion, leading with authority, and responding to needs with practical involvement. So we have a far better idea of what God is like, now that Jesus has shown us.

What this carol says strongly is that God does not stop being God in order to take on our human frame. Nether is Jesus just a good human or anointed prophet. The truth is that Jesus shares God's nature at the same time as taking on our human nature. He is 'God from God and Light from Light'.

All through Christian history this has been chewed over and analysed in an effort to understand it and express it in words. But, of course, the reason we get into tangles about it is that there are no words which can clearly express something totally outside our normal experience. Surely, we wonder, if a human is human, and God is God, then how can Jesus be both?

The disciples went on puzzling over it even after they had grasped that Jesus was the promised Messiah, God's anointed One, whom they had all been waiting for through the generations. When Jesus had asked them who they reckoned he was, Peter had spoken up and said, 'You are the Christ, the Son of the living God.' Yet just after Jesus has washed the disciples' feet and is soon to be arrested and crucified, they are still asking Jesus to show them the Father.

Jesus has to explain it to them once again, as he probably has to explain it to us over and over when the glazed look comes over our faces and we are making it all very complicated. Jesus expresses it simply by saying, 'I am in the Father and the Father is in me . . . It is the Father, living in me, who is doing his work.' And, after all, if being human and divine at once happened regularly, there would be nothing significant about it happening uniquely in the case of Jesus.

The wonderful advantage of the Christmas story is that we can relax about the cerebral rationalising and simply gaze at the baby who is Christ, the Lord. That's why, sprinkled between the verses of this great carol, is the chorus of faith and trusting worship: 'O come, let us adore him.'

DAY 7

Something to think, something to pray and something to do

Something to think . . .

Don't just sing the Christmas carols this year without them lingering in the spirit or the mind. Chew on them as you listen, so that the words release their flavour. Notice how they meditate on different aspects of the Christmas truth, and let them lead you into worship.

Something to pray . . .

What can I give him,
poor as I am?
If I were a shepherd
I would bring a lamb.
If I were a wise man
I would do my part.
Yet what *I* have I give him:
give my heart!

Something to do . . .

1 Sing a carol while you shower or walk, and listen to the words being sung to you.

2 Try writing a carol yourself that doesn't just use Christmas clichés but expresses what you are discovering about the meaning of Christmas.

3 Enjoy a carol service.

WEEK 4

FESTIVE FOOD AND DRINK

DAY 1

Choosing and preparing

We have arrived at the week before Christmas on this Advent journey, and it may well be that you are having to think about the festive food and drink now, because you are the one preparing it all or helping with the preparations. But even if you are in the happy position of having everything done for you this year, I hope you will still find something useful in this week's reflections!

Christmas dinner at the Cratchit household was goose with stuffing, 'eked out by the apple sauce and mashed potatoes' with gravy, and accompanied by 'some hot mixture in a jug with gin and lemons'. Afterwards came the pudding 'like a speckled cannon-ball so hard and firm, blazing in half of half-a-quatern of ignited brandy, and bedight with Christmas holly stuck into the top'. And after that was eaten, 'apples and oranges were put on the table, and a shovel-full of chestnuts on the fire'.

Charles Dickens seems to be relishing Christmas dinners he has enjoyed while he describes this one in *A Christmas Carol*! Traditions may seem set fast, but actually they shift and circle, and every year the magazines come out with glossy pictures of all kinds of different food and drink, according to your taste and diet.

So whereas at one time there wouldn't have been a great deal of choosing to do – you just provided what you were expected to provide – now there are endless choices to be made. We're almost spoilt for choice. And although that has a wonderful freedom to it, it's also typical of our whole lifestyle where even to buy a cup of coffee you need a three-page menu.

And there is actually more stress if there are constant choices to be made. We're so used to living like this that we take it for granted but maybe notice how relaxing it is on rare occasions when there is no choosing to be done. I wonder if it also subtly sets up in us the assumptions that we can select precisely what we want all the time, so that we become collectively less willing to compromise and give ourselves an ever-narrowing margin of error: if something isn't exactly what we want, it's regarded as completely wrong and useless.

That strikes me as being quite a destructive thought process to get into. Destructive for us individually because it has a long-term effect of chronic discontent, and collectively because community runs on compromises and a willingness to set down individual preferences in favour of the general needs. Perhaps we need to choose sometimes to care less about selecting precisely what we want, even in our prayer life; to fast from specifics and limit ourselves more and more to 'let your kingdom come and let your will be done, Lord, in this situation or that person'. At the same time, all the choosing proclaims our God-given ability to choose, and that's always worth celebrating because it is such a generous and courageous gift. By giving us the gift of choosing, God shows us, with great humility, extraordinary honour. Our God-given choosing presents us with the privilege of taking an active part in the direction of the world and the coming of God's kingdom.

As you choose what you are going to have for Christmas food and drink, you can celebrate this gift of free will which enables us to make choices all the time about everything, and pray for the grace to make good and wise choices, even if sometimes they are not our personal preference.

Let's go back to the Christmas menu and all the festive food and drink. Having made our main choices, we start preparing. If you are a cake and pudding maker, you may have done some of that preparation already. The stirring of that delicious, spicy Christmas pudding mixture is shared by everyone in our family still, with even the very youngest having their stir and a wish – but don't say what the wish is! And organised cake makers, among whom I am not numbered, will have their sweet-smelling cakes already settling and being fed at regular intervals with brandy.

There are turkeys to be ordered, endless shopping lists, and, when it comes to Christmas itself, the collecting, chopping, slicing, stuffing, marinating and so on. Spiritually it's the same. We make our big decision to be Christ followers, and then we join in the work of preparation for the coming of God's kingdom, the feast to which everyone is invited.

Together we work at those everyday chores of self-discipline and patience, loving service and thanksgiving, prayerful concern for one another and for the world. A lot of the work is kitchen rather than dining room jobs, but without it there would be no feast. It is like the root growth going on hidden in the earth before the plant can grow and produce its harvest fruit.

Loving people into the kingdom is like this as well. It's in the everyday, faithful availability to God and to one another that hearts get won for Christ. Church communities are there to be signs of the kingdom, communities of outreach and loving service, and it is the unremarkable but vital acts of friendliness, keeping in touch, noticing needs and providing practical help as well as prayer support, which speak to people of God's faithful and tender love.

As you do the waiting in checkout queues, preparing the Brussels sprouts and roast potatoes, rolling out pastry and filling mince pies, and all those other preparation jobs, make them all an act of loving prayer. Pray for those who have grown and harvested and sold everything. Thank God for the good earth and its harvest. Feel actively part of the workforce of Christ, privileged to be working together with Christians all over the world for the coming of the kingdom.

DAY 2

Ingredients and timing

Recipe books always include instructions for both ingredients and timing, because they are both of great importance in how the finished dish tastes. I confess that I am one of those who finds it almost impossible to obey recipes to the letter, and I'll often change or add to the ingredients on a whim. Sometimes it makes for a stunning success and sometimes turns a casserole into a disasterole.

Timing can make all the difference between squidgy and succulent, well done and burnt offering, risen and flat, crisp and teeth-shattering. There is a perfect moment to take the pie or cake out of the oven, and a perfect moment to bite into fresh warm bread.

I remember once baking the bread dough just as I left the house to pick up the children from school. In my foolish, Mr Bean way, I accidentally locked myself out and got back to the house smelling the bread cooking, while a neighbour helped with the children and I climbed a ladder to the balcony and managed to get in through a window. It all took some time and I was greatly relieved that when I reached the oven, there was the bread at that perfect moment for taking out!

God is always big on ingredients and timing. So often we experience the way different events and situations work together for good and surprise us by the wonderful way they produce blessing for many. In the middle of it, it can feel a bit like I felt struggling with the heavy ladder and working precariously at the window opening, and just hoping and praying something might be saved from my stupidity. But often I have found that our lovely God seems to understand our humanness and still works within some terrible situations of our own making to bring order and blessing, perhaps different now from the original plan, but nonetheless good and valuable.

Often my cry to God for help has been to put right things that have gone badly wrong because I didn't get the ingredients right. Ingredients like thoughtfulness or honesty or self-control. But God must be one of those creative chefs who sums up the situation and transforms it before it's too late. Like the kitchen servant at Hadden Hall, near Bakewell in Derbyshire, who had been told the ingredients for the pastry and accidentally left half of them out. Nothing daunted, she made these extra ingredients into a filling for the pastry case and created the Bakewell pudding, or tart, which is utterly delicious and well worth a visit to the pretty village of Bakewell!

I would recommend that you let God into your mistakes as early as possible, and watch how he transforms even impossible situations into blessing. We can truly taste and see that God is good. Remember that the end result is bound to be different from what you originally planned, so you have to be flexible and not a spiritually fussy eater. But you may well end up with something better and more satisfying than your first plan, simply because this redeemed recipe has the flavour of God in it.

And, yes, God is big on ingredients as well. We have been provided with a universe packed full of everything we need to sustain life, renew, recharge and heal. The planet Earth we know as home has great store cupboards of rain forests with their rich variety of roots, seeds, leaves and fruit. The present sea-bed and ancient sea-beds under deserts have preserved sunshine in the form of oil and coal and gas. The sun, waves and wind are full of renewable, sustainable power.

These are gifts. And we are to be stewards of such richness, properly ensuring that there is fair sharing and responsible management of them. We are not to squander unsustainable resources on an indulgent spending spree which will leave future generations in need. We are not to pay unrealistically low prices for harvests of tea, coffee and chocolate which others have laboured for, so that they can barely survive and we can relax in our unthreatened wealth.

As Christ followers we need to be right at the front of the campaign for just and fair trade, working at changing systems to improve living and working conditions, even though that means paying more realistic prices ourselves. We should be there at the forefront of using renewable energy, in our homes and churches, and be properly wary of any power that may leave a legacy of radioactive waste for future generations to cope with. We should be living as simply as we can, with as light a footprint on the earth as possible, even if that means looking again at our means of transport and general lifestyle.

The thing that will kick-start us into actually doing something about all of this is love. If we take the trouble to find out what the effects of our actions are on so many of the world's poor, if we listen to their stories and ask uncomfortable questions, our hearts will hurt us into taking these issues seriously. Seriously enough to change how we live.

As you choose your ingredients this Christmas, bear all this in mind, and choose with love for the earth and its peoples. Read the labels and notice who is getting most of the money for what you are buying, and whether or not it is fair to the growers. Notice how far the goods have travelled, and try to cut down on air mileage by buying more locally.

Look at each ingredient as the wonderful gift it is, thanking God for the good earth and enjoying the shapes, colours, textures and variety of creation.

DAY 3

Laying the table

A beautifully laid table is all part of a festive celebration and has a marvellous air of expectancy about it: food will soon be coming!

My dad used to come home weary after work and a long journey and because he was in a lot of pain I remember his face looking grey as he hauled himself up the stairs to our flat. My mum always made a point of having the table laid ready for him to eat. She reckoned that was an important part of the welcome, and she'd get food on it as soon as possible, but somehow the laid table was a sign of hope and love, and I'm sure she was right. It did help.

Many years later, when I used to creep into the candlelit church for a midweek evening Communion service, and I was tired after coming straight from my shift at work, I remember feeling that same loving and careful welcome of the table laid with a freshly laundered white cloth, candles burning, and the bread, wine and water all ready. I was conscious of Jesus inviting us personally to a special meal in his presence. The air of quiet expectancy was there, and started its refreshing work on my soul and body straightaway.

When we eat out it's partly to avoid the cooking and washing up and partly to enjoy the setting of a particular restaurant. That laying of the table and the general ambiance is all part of the price you are charged and feel it's worthwhile paying. Our local Indian restaurant has recently been refurbished, with intimate lighting and a quality feel to the table settings, and it's made quite a difference to custom. More people are choosing to eat there now, even though the food was always excellent.

The way we prepare for worship in church is like laying the table. If possible, we need to finish all our preparations earlier and have the holy space set up and welcoming as we take time to pray. In the prison where I am chaplain we have started having an evening Communion service which begins as soon as the prisoners are unlocked for evening association. That means none of them is available for the setting up, and I find it a real privilege to do that table-laying for them on this occasion, setting up an atmosphere in our little chapel with lots of candlelight, quiet music, and the beautiful but simply laid altar table. The lights are low and I pray for them all by name before they arrive.

Then God blesses the laid table with his lovely, healing gift of grace. The women talk of this as their special oasis of peace in the week, and God's presence is tangible. The Spirit guides us to do the urgent work of prayer because we are attentive, and we all find it humbling that in this place of locked doors we experience the freedom of God's people. We leave quietened, healed, forgiven and fed, and I love to see God's serenity on their faces.

What is true for church can also be true of our times of personal prayer. Many faiths take seriously their prayers in the home, and people have a shrine or something of natural beauty as a focus. In our Christian homes that tradition has almost disappeared and we find ourselves praying secretly in bed, well away from the rest of the family, with the Christmas crib the only time of year that there is a focus for prayer.

I wonder what signals this gives to our children and those who visit our homes? Is it so odd to suggest that in Christian homes we might start laying a table which is a focus for regular prayer? If that became more usual, what would you choose to put on your table or small space?

I think I would have some flowers or leaves or shells – something from the natural world to remind me to be thankful. And there might be a fresh white cloth with a candle and a cross, or a small icon or prayer. Perhaps I would change the mood and colour according to the church seasons. Perhaps the week's Collect would be included.

Christianity, like Judaism, is really a home-based faith, and I think we have pulled it away from homes with the effect of it ceasing to be a visibly natural part of our whole daily life. Perhaps this Advent we could all start a new habit of laying a table or a small space like this and re-consecrate our homes as places of prayer and daily worship.

One table we still lay sometimes is the dining table for festive meals at home. At Christmas there are often more people around the table than usual, as family members make the effort to share the meal together. Laying the table for such an occasion can be a great opportunity for prayer.

Pray for each person as their place at the table is laid. Pray in thankfulness, calling to mind the qualities and characteristics that you value in them. Simply voicing these to yourself softens your heart towards them, if there are sometimes tensions or disagreements between you.

Think about decoration for each place setting and for the table centre, dressing the table so that it reflects God's welcome and Christmas joy. As you do it, ask God's blessing on the mealtime conversations, and invite Jesus to be there, since the meal is, after all, in his honour.

DAY 4

Eating together

The statistics show that we don't tend to make a regular habit of eating together on a daily basis. Breakfast is more often a rushed slice of toast or bowl of cereal, eaten standing in the kitchen or between other jobs. Or there are different shifts of breakfast as each member of the household approaches their time to leave the house or stay and do the clearing up. And in the evening the shift system carries on, according to who has to be out again.

Many families try to make sure that everyone sits down and eats together at least once a week. Traditionally that was at Sunday lunch, and although the timing of the meal and what we eat at it changes over the years, there is still a commitment to that, even if not every week. Pubs and restaurants and take-aways do a good trade in catering for busy people who recognise the value of sitting down together and eating.

The word 'companion' originally meant 'bread sharer'. It's easy to see how a bread sharer took on the present meaning of companion. If someone is your companion, it suggests there is an easy, relaxed, comfortable relationship between you. You enjoy being in each other's company and can chat amicably about things dear to your heart, as well as spending some times without needing to say anything at all. We talk about a 'companionable silence', don't we?

You can imagine that kind of relationship developing between bread sharers: those who share food together. They might be travelling together and break some bread between them on the way. Or they might share bread because they work or live together and have got used to each other's ways.

Jesus chose the context of a meal – bread sharing – at which to meet his disciples in a special way in every place and generation. The Jewish Passover he and his friends were celebrating, at that last meal taken before Jesus' arrest and crucifixion, was a family meal, reliving the experience of the last meal eaten in slavery in Egypt before the escape through the Red Sea. The original Passover was eaten in a frame of mind more like our usual breakfasts. 'You are to eat it quickly, for you are to be dressed for travel, with your sandals on your feet . . .' Sounds familiar!

But as the Jewish people remembered and relived their amazing rescue story, the meal became a very practical, hands-on form of worship, and families down the generations gathered to sit down and eat Passover together. That's what Jesus was doing with his friends that evening. When, as part of the Passover meal, he took bread and blessed, broke and shared it, and shared the cup of wine, saying it was like a new covenant, his disciples would have started to understand what Jesus was about to do in the context of rescue from slavery and being led into a new freedom.

At every Communion, that last supper of the Passover meal goes on and on. We share bread and wine not only with Jesus but with every other Christ follower in the whole of time and space. It's a bit like the feeding of the five thousand, where Jesus directed the people to sit down in their different groups of about fifty, and he went on blessing and breaking and sharing the bread and fish until every person had been provided with sufficient feeding. I like to think of our church gatherings as extra groups of people on the grass, all part of the same meal where Jesus is feeding us.

One of the Eucharistic prayers talks of Jesus as 'the living bread, in whom all our hungers are satisfied'. And this is a communal experience of a gathered community, rather than something to do on our own. Communion is like those occasions when we recognise the value of sitting and eating together, at a meal of cosmic significance.

Christmas dinner is in our culture rather like the Jewish Passover meal. We make quite a significant effort to be together in our family and household groups on that day. We try and make sure that everyone who wants to share the eating together will be able to do so. There are special Christmas meals put on by volunteers for those who are homeless or those living alone, because something makes us sense the importance of being gathered at a meal as we celebrate Christmas.

All age groups are included and once all the preparations have been done there's the happiness of looking around the table at all the faces, with stories and jokes to be told, and good food to share. Quality time. Time to spend with one another in a relaxed and pleasant way. Even if there are family tensions and for the rest of the year there's bickering, it's as if our dream for eating together at Christmas is different. We want to make the effort to rise above those tensions and get on with one another.

The good food and drink certainly helps. With our bodies being well fed and filled with delicious tastes, we are in a better frame of mind to be tolerant and forgiving, less likely to fly off the handle and let arguments build. Although it is true that family splits happen more often at Christmas than at any other time of year, it is also true that for most families in any one year the Christmas meal is when relationships are deepened and often healed, tensions soothed and memories built up of enjoying one another's company.

Always invite Jesus to your meals. He is a good guest to have at dinner parties of any kind – and especially at Christmas!

DAY 5

We are what we eat and drink

My two-year-old grandchild was stretched out over the floor playing. It wasn't that long ago that I could fit her into the crook of one arm! She was enjoying thinking that all the new length of her body is made from milk, bread and Marmite, fish fingers and baked beans, chicken and chocolate. What a splendid system that converts food and drink into energy and body cells! It's true: we are what we eat and drink.

Research has shown that school performance in children can be improved by diet, and learning impaired by poor nutrition. So at present there is quite a drive to improve the quality of what our children eat. Many schools have switched to 'fruit only' snacks, and there is advice about how to prepare a healthy packed lunch which the children are prepared to eat.

Look at the vitamin shelves to see how that market has increased too. There are cocktails of vitamins and minerals to suit every lifestyle, so as to ensure that we all get enough of what we need to be in tip-top condition, however rushed or stressed our lives are. It rather assumes that none of us is likely to be eating a good all-round diet, so we're bound to need the supplements.

There is a darker side to this as well. With the BSE scare we suddenly woke up to the fact that there are health implications of eating cattle fed unnaturally on animal derivatives and pumped with routine antibiotics. Suddenly we realised that we need to look with much more responsibility at how we farm, whether animals, fish or crops. The quick, short-term gains are possibly laying down long-term dangers.

It all makes us look at what we eat and drink in a different way. We are beginning to walk around the supermarket peering more conscientiously at the labels on our food. Is it organic? Does it contain too much salt, sugar or fat? Were dolphins endangered by the fishermen catching this tuna? Did the cocoa, tea and coffee growers get a fair deal through this particular brand? Will the planet be badly affected by the marketing or packaging of this item? How much fuel was used to transport these plums or cucumbers? Were the chickens that laid these eggs able to range freely and were they responsibly looked after?

So many questions, you have to allow extra time for reading labels and making choices!

But thank goodness we are facing up to these responsibilities more. At one time you were considered distinctly odd to be bothered about any of this, and only a few would make their views known to local shops. Thank goodness that there are real vegetarian options on menus now, rather than the pile of grated cheese to replace the meat. Thank goodness there is a more widespread concern for the care of the planet and its creatures and plants.

We are what we eat and drink, not just physically but spiritually as well. Part of recognising that we are given this remarkable planet as our home and its resources to share and care for is that we have to do our very best to share and care for in a way that honours God. Having fairly traded refreshments after worship becomes part of the worship. Checking what and how much goes into our bodies as food and drink is part of our worship, since our bodies are temples of God's Holy Spirit.

While we are becoming more responsible in choosing what we eat and drink, there is a widespread drugs and alcohol culture which ought to make us concerned. A high proportion of all crime is drugs- and alcohol-related, and mental health is also noticeably affected. I find it alarming to talk with so many in prison whose thinking or sleeping has been disrupted permanently as a result of drugs damage. Voices in their heads which they cannot shut out, severe depression and so on – terrible conditions to live with in a normal way.

Plenty of people know they drink too much than is good for them but use it as self-medication. It's an off switch to the memory or the inhibitions or the worries. Unfortunately, such self-medicating has dangerous side effects. And it never helps cure the real underlying problem, but simply adds to it and prevents us from addressing it.

If we are fearful that we are basically unacceptable and unlovable, it's quite possible that we use food or drink or drugs to muffle those fears. Sadly, once the hit has gone, we feel worse than ever and get ourselves into a downward spiral which turns addictive.

What is God's medicine for a fearful heart that is convinced it is unacceptable and unlovable? What is God's medicine for a worried, anxious mind and ghosts from the past?

The spiritual food and drink of God's loving acceptance of each of us personally, his ongoing concern for our well-being, and his grace to heal us through forgiveness. And, yes, there are side effects of this medicine as well. They are peace and joy.

DAY 6

Crackers

There they are at each place setting at the Christmas meal, waiting to be snapped with a bang so the contents drop out on to the floor and set you grovelling for the paper hat, awful joke and plastic ring or toy. No Christmas party is complete without everyone from Grandpa to the baby wearing a coloured paper crown, at least until it splits or falls over the eyes or drops into the custard.

Your memory links them with that slightly uncomfortable but pleasant over-full feeling and the relaxed stage of the meal when sleep is wanting to catch up on you!

I wanted us to think of crackers in this last reflection of Advent because of the way they contain the exciting 'bang!', something to read, a hat to wear and something to do. One Christmas we had some crackers which all held whistles of different notes, together with music, so everyone could attempt 'Jingle bells' and 'Rudolph'.

At first it's all hidden from view, and it's the surprise of the cracker that spills everything out. Well, I've often found that God is fond of surprising us when we are ready to work with him. It's hard to pull a cracker on your own – the whole fun is in two of you pulling in different directions in a co-ordinated way. Often it's as if God has placed a cracker by our plate, and we sit and look at it rather than entering into that relationship of co-ordinated tension with God.

Jacob had run away from his twin brother Esau after cheating him of his father's blessing, and is on his way back, full of anxiety about how Esau will receive him. In his sleep he relives that wrestle of feelings, begging for blessing. He is asked his name, just as his father had asked him all those years ago. That time Jacob had lied that he was Esau. This time he honestly replies that he is Jacob – and, interestingly, the name means 'cheat'. But there is healing out of the wrestling: 'Your name will no longer be Jacob (cheat). You have struggled with God and with men, and you have won; so your name will be Israel (he struggles with God)' (Genesis 32:28).

We don't tend to equate conflict and wrestling with healing and reconciliation, but in God's economy that's exactly what happens. When we engage with God, the peace we are given is not a false, temporary muffling of our deep-seated wounds and worries, but a creative tension which draws us to a controlled 'crack!' and out come the hidden gifts, which were previously inaccessible. God knows what he is doing. Surgery is sharp but necessary for healing. Honesty in facing our darker places in God's company releases the grace God gives to deal with them.

Even the little crack of a cracker needs to be treated with respect. We have to keep it away from the eyes in case it hurts. And there is the sharp noise of it, meant to alarm in a fun way. God is wanting to engage with us seriously and God is not to be fooled. At the moment of real engagement, we sense the power of God and respect it. 'The fear of God is the beginning of wisdom' (Psalm 111:10).

The words which become clear from that wrestling with God may be a bit like a riddle which you have to work on to understand fully. It may be a phrase or verse from scripture which suddenly has new meaning and immediacy for you. It may even be funny. I remember feeling panicky about how I was going to manage a whole hour of a difficult situation and letting God in on the panic. I kind of heard his wry smile as he spoke into my heart the lovely way God does: 'I promise I'll only give you one moment at a time.' And I laughed and felt less anxious straightaway. Even I could manage it moment by moment.

The crown which becomes available to us is like the status God gives us that we can wear proudly. We are sons and daughters of the King of love. Invisibly we wear it, knowing that everything we do, think and say is affected by our wearing of it. To know we are loved and lovable and acceptable and accepted – to *really* know it – is a powerful force of healing and blessing, not only for us but for anyone we communicate with when behaving in character.

Often such an encounter with God results in a commission: we are given something to do or work with. And we might look at it sceptically, turning it this way and that and wishing it was something else. Try thanking God for it, however unlike your expectation God's commission for you is. I have known people convinced they are called in a particular direction and when they have been shown a different path they just can't bring themselves to accept it, and they shut down on all ministry, in a kind of spiritual sulk. That seems sad because God's sovereign will for us is full of blessing, and yes, it may well surprise us or look inferior to us at first until we start getting involved. Then gradually we begin to see why God has given this commission for us, and the blessing to us and others can be released. I have known various commissions which, to be honest, looked nothing but trouble to me and not at all what I wanted to be doing. But I am so very thankful that I did them, because out of them I can see blessing has come – God was actually setting up a blessing to me and others, and there I was almost shutting it off before it could happen.

We're back to Mary and Joseph again, aren't we? They were prepared to engage with God, honour his authority and respect his plans for them. They were given the instructions: 'You shall call him Jesus (which means Saviour).' Simeon spoke his riddles of prophecy which came true. And suddenly they were parenting the Son of God, bringing him up in their household with all the challenge and blessing of a situation they could never have imagined.

DAY 7

Something to think, something to pray and something to do

Something to think . . .

As you enjoy all the festive food and drink this Christmas, thank God for his rich provision, for the good earth and its fruits. May the Christmas meal be one where Jesus is the invisible but honoured guest, ready to heal and restore, to join in the fun and start conversations.

Something to pray . . .

A grace to say at your Christmas dinner:

Lord Jesus, born in Bethlehem
on the first Christmas Day,
welcome to this meal with us.
We give thanks to God for food on the table
and for the love and fellowship we share.
As we eat and drink to celebrate Christmas,
may we know your love in our hearts.
Amen.

Something to do . . .

1 Enjoy your Christmas as a great celebration of God choosing to share our human nature and show us in person what God is like.

2 Let the bright joy of Christmas go on shining in you even after you have thrown out the tree.

3 Become a fair-trade household as a practical thank-you.